RICH COACH POOR COACH

How to BE a 6-figure coach, have time to travel, enjoy your family, and love your life.

SABASTIAN SANG HUYNH

Copyright

All rights reserved.

© 2016 Sabastian Huynh

No part of this publication may be copied, reproduced in any format, by any means, electronic or otherwise, without prior consent from the copyright owner of this book.

Sabastian Huynh

Published in the United States

Contents

Dedication iv

Introduction xi

Chapter 1: Your Come From 1

Chapter 2: You Are In 11

Chapter 3: You Can 20

Chapter 4: You Count 33

Chapter 5: Your Why 45

Chapter 6: Your Comfort Zone 59

Chapter 7: Your Fears 69

Chapter 8: You The Artist 79

Chapter 9: Your Process 89

Dedication

Love never gives up. Love cares more for others than for self. Love puts up with anything. Trusts God always, always looks for the best, never looks back, but keeps going to the end. 1 Corinthians 13.

The reality of you reading this book is nothing short of a miracle. I have overcome the fear of rejection and you hold in your hands a gift of that journey. I could never have gotten here without my bride, Donna, of over 20 years believing that I am a gift to the world and supporting me to BE-ing that gift. Thank you babe for your endless support and belief in me.

I stand on the shoulders of many men and women who have gone before me, whom I draw all my principles from and acknowledge there is nothing new in these pages, only principles that work. Principles that I have personally tried, owned and found success in. These principles I will pass down to my children, and they to their children, which will empower them to live a life of freedom. This book is dedicated to Kaleb, Joshua, Seth and Selah. Know that your lives are created to give away, to contribute to the universal story of love and to leave your fingerprints everywhere.

Finally, I accredit my transformation and passion to serve others to a defining moment when I accepted the sweet, gentle and persistent invitation from Jesus to trust my life was created for more then I was living for. Understanding I was created with a purpose, I invite you to discover that you are more then you could ever imagine. And when you lead yourself through this journey from your comfort zone to your committed goal, you will be able to consistently lead others and produce a sustainable six-figure life style as a coach.

My hero, The Apostle Paul said

The defeated, the demoralized- whoever. I didn't take on their way of life. I kept my bearing in Christ- but I entered their world and tried to experience things from their point of view.

I've become just about every sort of servant there is in my attempts to lead those I meet into a God-saved life.

> **BE what is missing, then others will BE a contribution on the canvas of life.**

Personal Note:

1. This Book Is For Everyone, Not Only Coaches

The first four chapters are foundational for a six-figure coach! However, it's not just for coaches. I believe you will be purchasing this book for your friends, family and client just for them to read the first four chapters.

In fact, my little secret of being a successful six-figure coach is that I constantly reinforce these principles with my clients throughout our coaching journey. So why not just buy them the book, set a solid foundation for your relationship and use it as a base camp for your coaching journey. You will be going back to these principles over and over again, that's if you're following my method of BE-ing a six-figure coach.

Personally you will see how these principles of having an abundant mindset - that you're already "in", you "can" and you "count" - will transform your marriage, parenting, friendships and all your personal relationships.

2. I Will Be Descriptive And Never Prescriptive

I believe another "secret" of my success of being a six-figure coach is my transparency, authenticity and congruency. These three ways of BE-ing are another book within themselves. So to keep it simple here, I am who I am and the journey it took for me to get here is what is available to you to be a six-figure coach. I have to be congruent with my beliefs, world view and experiences. I share them openly and never prescribe them to be your beliefs or world views. For example, I have faith in a God who created the heavens and earth. It is fundamental to me and the way I live my life.

I believe in only one absolute truth and everything else is grey and negotiable, and the world is to big for me to speak from certainty. So if I share my experiences from my faith, I will never prescribe it to you or in any way elevate my self above others who do not have the same beliefs. I share to drive a point home and only when it will benefit you to BEcome a six-figure coach.

3. Application Is Transformation

Here is an example of me being transparent. I firmly believe in this ancient scripture from the Apostle James:

But don't just listen to God's word. ***You must do what it says****. Otherwise, you are only fooling yourselves. For if you listen to the word and don't obey, it is like glancing at your face in a mirror. You see yourself, walk away, and forget what you look like.* ***But if you look carefully into the perfect law that sets you free, and if you do what it says and don't forget what you heard, then God will bless you for doing it.***

Though this is talking about your relationship with God, the principle is APPLICATION. If you read everything I tell you to "BE" and you don't apply it, then you will understand why you're not a six-figure coach. BE-ing a six-figure coach has less to do with program, process, procedures, tools, and tricks. Though these support and accelerate your coaching, the most transformational part of your coaching and getting your clients results is found in your way of "BE-ing." You will set the container for your clients, family, and friends to experiment and fail forward.

Only when you APPLY what I teach you here will you have the rewards that come with BE-ing a six-figure coach.

4. Resist the Temptation!

If you're truly a six-figure coach, you will want to jump right into the coaching model and skip the first several chapters. I understand and DON'T DO IT!!! This is not a traditional how to coach, color-by-number coaching system. To BE a six-figure coach, it takes more then a simple coaching model, it takes your way of BE-ing. Grab a glass of your favorite beverage, sit in a place you won't be interrupted and complete the first several chapters that set the foundation for the coaching model. THEN pause, and meditate on those principles. Challenge yourself if you can embrace this way of BE-ing. Then dive into the coaching principles.

Yes, you will get some benefit from reading just the coaching principles. But you will receive the full advantage if you read in order and let the principles build off of one another.

Your Way Of BE-ing

A. Your Come From

B. You Are In

C. You Can

D. You Count

Coaching Foundations Of A Six-Figure Coach

1. Your Why

2. Your Comfort Zone

3. Your Fears

4. You The Artist

Introduction

"If you don't like change, you're going to like irrelevance even less!"

General Shinseki

Here's the challenge. First, coaching is not a regulated industry, so right now, there's no benchmark for what a great coach, a good coach and an average coach is. So how do we know who is a great coach? Who's worthy of making six figures? Who's worthy of your time and attention? Who will help you get your results? The challenge is we're coming into an industry that's not regulated, and you have to make a huge noise to be recognized, and the only way to make noise in this industry is to create results for your clients. Second, there's no standard of excellence. Third, there's no practical way to get your name out there because there's no benchmark for them to measure you against. Fourth, marketing costs an exorbitant amount of money to get your name out there. Then, fifth, if you are part of any certification industry, you already limit yourself to be a part of any other coaching industry because then your certification may go against the other certifications that they're looking for. So the challenge is that we're in the wild wild west of coaching. There's no standard. There are no prerequisites. There are no accepted procedures. There's no right of passage. We have no indicators to know if you're a great coach.

What's the benchmark? What's the standard besides getting your clients' results, and then marketing those results in a way that position you to be a known coach and worthy of the price that you charge?

This leads to the ultimate challenge, most coaches don't make six-figures! Regardless of the coaching system available or the amount of money you spend on marketing your services, there is the invisible ceiling that we continually hit and the six-figure income with the life style that it provides is visible, yet some how out of our reach.

The world is changing. Those who want to advance their career need coaching. They need people who can see their blind spots and who are willing to call it out, who are willing to say what no one else will say, that's very obvious to everyone except for the leader who's advancing their life. They also need coaches who can inspire them to be the best version of themselves, who see the best version of them and will call them forth into that best version when they're playing anything less or smaller.

The world is changing. The leaders who are advancing their career and lives and advancing society to the next level need coaches that could call forth that leader out of their comfort zone and into their vision, invite them in a way that inspires them and reminds them that their vision is bigger than themselves.

No longer are mentors, counselors and consultants needed. No longer are those specialized industries of value because we are no longer the traditional paths of leadership. In fact, entrepreneurs these days are not following traditional paths. Entrepreneurs these days are leading the way and they're taking shortcuts and hacks, and they're not taking a traditional route. So what the leaders are looking for are coaches. They need coaches who have experience in getting results for themselves and for others. They need coaches who have gone through the trials and the tribulations of life, who've learned to overcome obstacles, and most importantly, overcome the mental barriers and hurdles. They're looking for coaches, not consultants, mentors or counselors with degrees, but who lack experience to overcome challenges or lack proven results.

The world is changing. The old model of business is going out the door. Leaders no longer are doing things themselves any longer. In fact, the world is changing so that no longer do leaders constantly work harder and do more to get results. Information technology is everywhere. The old model of just putting your head down, nose to the grind, and do, do, and do more no longer works, because the more they do, they still can't get enough in this technology age to get the results they need to become significant, and to make things happen in their world.

Therefore coaching is needed. True coaching is coaching that calls forth leaders into unprecedented space. Invites them to new beliefs and exposes their limited beliefs. Coaching that comes from a coach who has been personally transformed. Coaching that doesn't depend on a simple formula or fancy tools. The coaching that is needed comes from a foundational place that is universal and can transform all humanity regardless of culture or ethnicity. This type of coaching will give you a six-figure life style!

The old model is that you have to do more and work harder to reach your goal. Leaders used to roll up their sleeves, get people to do it with them, and the harder they worked, the longer hours, the more they would have. Here's the funny part. The more they had, the bigger business, the more employees, more investment - it still wasn't enough. They couldn't reach the point that the business owner would be significant, be happy, and be satisfied. Then they'd start that vicious cycle over again. You would do more and more and more and more, so you could have more to show your status. Then your status wasn't big enough to the person next to you, so you would do more and more and more. You never became significant, important, or achieved your dream because you had a moving target on what your dream was. The world is changing. No longer can you do more so we can have more, and then you will become significant and important one day. Elbow grease will not get you to become the six-figure coach you're committed to being.

The new model is that entrepreneurs are taking over, and traditional business models, and business leaders, are becoming archaic. Traditional, old ways, was to grind it out, put your head down, work hard, do so that one day you will have enough then you will become important. When you are enough, then you can take a seat back and become significant, and important, and enjoy it. Unfortunately, we've seen generations pass us, who never arrived, never became enough. All they did was work more, more, and more. They would have some material possessions to show for their success; a big house, luxury cars, and corner office, but those things still would not be enough, so you would work more and harder to only make another lap around the hamster wheel.

Maybe you have an area in your life where it's satisfying, like work. You hit milestones, goals, and have some achievements. But in your personal life, you're wrestling and struggling with your marriage or parenthood. Maybe you still haven't gotten married. Because you haven't done enough yet and haven't established a six-figure income, so you are not significant enough to get married.

Now, in this new model, you're not following the traditional ways. You're coming from a place that you're already significant. You come from a place with a purpose that was birthed within you. You're coming from a place that you are already significant, and you have a purpose and you're working from of that purpose. Whatever you do is aligned with your purpose. Then, whatever you do gives you what you have, and you're content with what you have. No longer do you have these ambitions to have things that make you significant.

What you have now, or desire now, are more relational or collaborative concepts. You want to have a peace of mind when you go home; what you do contributes something greater than to yourself. This new model, the world's faster, technology's making information available 24-7. You could get technology anywhere you want, anytime you want.

In fact, my last visit to Korea was the most amazing experience of technology. From getting off the airplane in Korea throughout my entire experience there, I had Wi-Fi connection, free Wi-Fi connection at that. All the way from the airport into the city of Seoul, you couldn't go anywhere that you would lose a free internet connection. Technology is available 24-7. Technology king, but the application of technology is the ruler of the land of unlimited possibilities. The application is what's needed these days, of this free technology.

Sifting through the technology is also needed. Knowing what technology will support your end goal, your vision, and your "come from." In this new model, entrepreneurs are even younger. They're not traditional college graduates. They're very passionate, they work off their pain, and they see the issues in this society they want to resolve. These entrepreneurs are less experienced in holistic side of life, but they're very experienced at one niche that they're pursuing. They have one niche area that they're passionate about, and they're being very successful in.

I have a friend I've known since he was 18. He's in his mid 30's now. He started off just trying to figure out what's purpose in life, and he started selling online products on eBay and Amazon. Several years later, he's making over ten million a year selling products on the Internet. The technology is faster. Clients are younger, less experienced, they didn't go to business school, and they don't have a MBA, but they are focused on that niche they are in. They have so much experience and knowledge in that niche, but they are less experienced in the holistic picture of business and that is why they need a coach.

The new model is also about collaboration. Because people are so focused on their niche, they're collaborating with people outside their bubble, and they need a coach to support them on whom they need to collaborate with. They need coaching to navigate in these new collaborative spaces, and relationships.

This new model has higher stakes for everyone involved. These new entrepreneurs' failures are public. There's nothing hidden in the social media culture that they live in. They live with higher anxiety, and higher tension of their mistakes that they're not proud of. These entrepreneurs are more collaborative, but whom do they collaborate with? Who can they rely on, who has proven results that they can collaborate with? These failures, that these entrepreneurs are wrestling with, no longer affect them self, but they affect a community of people. They affect those who they have to collaborate with. They affect partners they are doing business with. They affect their family they return home to daily. They affect the non-profit they support.

This new model is different from the traditional business models, traditional MBAs, and the good ol' boy clubs used to work. This new model, it's faster. Technology available 24-7. Entrepreneurs are younger, they're less experienced, more collaborative, needing more support and coaching. The stakes are higher. Failure is no longer private, but public, because of social media. Their failure has a ripple effect in the community that they're in.

The new model of business requires a coach. An outside voice, outside pair of eyes, outside commitment to the business owner's success, to the leader's success. The new model is to have a coach, who's not in it, and blinded by the everyday problems, but beside you, turning your complaints into commitments. The new model is having someone who has proven results in their own life, having tools to help you have self-awareness, identify issues and barriers, and stay focused on your vision. To introduce you to, and help qualify, those that you will collaborate with. The new model is about having a coach who has a stake in the game with you, meaning your success is your coach's success. This coach in the new world of business has more then a bag of tools. They have a unique way of BE-ing.

My quick success story of being a coach. I didn't become a coach overnight because I knew that's what I wanted to do. I didn't become a coach because there was a financial goal that it would give me. I didn't become a coach because of the flexibility to coach anybody from around the world via the phone. I didn't become a coach because I enjoy celebrating other people's victory, because when they succeeded, I succeeded.

I didn't become a coach because it gave me a lifestyle where not only am I coaching people to professional excellence and achieving their goals and rewards, and I can use those exact same principles to coach my wife and my kids into their vision so they help me personally and professionally. I didn't become a coach for all those reasons.

My quick story is I got frustrated as a leader and business owner. I got tired of failing. I got tired of hitting the invisible ceiling where I self-sabotaged myself. So I went on my own personal journey and I asked the questions that got me where I'm at today as a six-figure coach. I asked the question, "Why do leaders and entrepreneurs get frustrated and quit?" Why have I aborted so many start ups and failed at multiple business opportunities? Why have I self-sabotaged myself from collaborating and partnering with certain people who could have taken my business to the next level?

I asked the questions and I resolved my own issues. When I resolved my own issues, I realized I'm sitting on gold. I'm sitting on something that could save other people thousands of hours, and days and years of effort. Not including the thousands and ten thousands of dollars I've lost in all my business ventures and false starts.

Today I am a coach because I resolved my own issues. I realized I have a calling bigger than creating a business for myself and a lifestyle for my family. Instead, I have a purpose to support other leaders and entrepreneurs to overcome those barriers: mental, physical and spiritual barriers that limited them from BE-ing successful leaders and entrepreneurs. I realize in order to be the significant business owner I always dreamt of being, I had to give it away.

My success story is not about how to become a coach. My story is about how I found the secret of being a successful business leader and entrepreneur. The realization is that to become successful, I couldn't focus just on myself, but I needed to give it away to the world.

It Will Work For You!

The most exciting part about my story is that it's just not my story, it's possible for you and you can do it, too. See, that's what took me so long to get where I am. Intuitively I knew how to get myself out of certain situations and then I'd build success from failure, on top of another failure, on top of another failure, and finally, I achieved my dream. Then I took a step back and I looked. What were the common milestones that I hit in these mental, physical, emotional, spiritual barriers? When I captured those milestones, I saw a process and through that process, I saw steps that anyone could replicate. It's not just my story. This is going to be your story. You could do it, too. You can be a 6-figure coach. You can enjoy life, supporting other people to achieve their dreams because you're going to first do it for yourself. You have to pass your mental, emotional, physical, and spiritual barriers, because when your clients hit those areas, you've been there first. Now maybe not in the exact same way, but the principles you used to break through your barriers are the same principles you will share with them.

It's not just my story, this coaching journey is for you also. I'm going to give you a step-by-step replicable framework and model that you'll be able to reproduce in your life and become a 6-figure coach. It's possible. Don't listen to that's just for Sabastian. That it's just his story. My story that has a process, procedures, and steps. A framework. It will turn into your story because you'll be able to do it also.

Here're the reasons why you should keep reading. I'm going to take you through a process that's intertwined with personal stories and testimonies of success, but they're going to be laid out in such a way that not only does it flow and make sense, but also it'll build one step on top of another. Then you're going to be able to instantly apply these principles to your own life. As you apply these principles to your own life and get results for yourself, you'll be able to get results for your clients. But you should keep reading only if you're serious about having a personal transformation in your life so you can give it away and live a six-figure coaching lifestyle.

Then, as you get a personal transformation in your life, you'll be able to give it away to others in this amazing framework, process, and step-by-step model I'll give you. Here's another reason you should keep on reading. Because you'll find out that you're able to find some kind of extra-supernatural energy and life when you walk with someone and help them achieve their dreams and goal, even if it's not your dream or goal, as long as it's not immoral or evil and you could align with it.

Another reason you should keep on reading. If you want a lifestyle where you value your time, and your creativity is not locked in from a 9 to 5, coaching is the perfect vehicle to do so. You can be with your clients from anywhere around the world. I have coached people who were in the United States of America while I was on vacation with my family in Thailand. I have coached people in California while I was in New York, coached people in Florida while I was in Colorado. Where I was located when I coached them didn't matter.

You should keep on reading if you want some time to enjoy your family, where you can spend quality time and take intermediate breaks to go and coach someone. You should keep reading if you want a lifestyle that you enjoy what you do because you know you make an impact in the world, and your vision's bigger than yourself, and the people that you're transforming are transforming other people that you couldn't touch. That's why you should keep on reading because this book is not about me. This book is not about you. This book is about the world and our contribution to it.

CHAPTER 1

Your Come From

"To the person who does not know where he wants to go, there is no favorable wind."

Seneca, Roman philosopher

Can you relate to waking up in the morning and clumsily turning off the alarm clock with your eyes half open? Forcing yourself out of your warm cozy bed to the cold floor. The first thought in your mind is about that hot cup of coffee to kick start your day. Then the next thought, which isn't so comforting, "Oh no, here we go again." A flood of concerns flows through your head about yesterday's problems that are yet to be resolved. Having to deal with people who are on your "avoid" list. Evading dealing with their issues or hearing their complaints. Endless meetings you're dreading since they go nowhere and are a waste of your time. So by that time you get to the only bright part of your day, the cup of coffee. You're ready to crawl back into your bed hoping it was only a nightmare and you could wake up without yesterday's problems. Then reality kicks in after your first sip of the hot, soothing, and aromatic coffee. It's not a nightmare and this cup of coffee will be the best part of your day.

Our mornings don't have to be so hopeless. Our morning can be full of excitement and anticipation of something great. Our mornings can be like Christmas morning daily! Remember how full of excitement and anticipation Christmas morning was? How you didn't know what you would get and regardless of what it was going to be, you would love it. Those mornings come from a commitment to create an adventure out of whatever you got. Usually you knew in general what you would have gotten because you asked for it, requested it, and in my case begged for it. We will talk in the later chapters on how to have the excitement of Christmas morning daily! For now, let understand why we barely get out of bed and our greatest anticipation is that cup of coffee.

Your attitude when you wake up is based normally from your history. Your past experience of yesterday, last week, last month and sometimes events from years past. I call it your "come from." Where do you come from when you enter a conversation? Where you usually come from is your past history, your past possibilities, your past failures, your past success. Those things are usually what you bring into a conversation in the moment. In the same way, your morning is filled with your own conversations about how today will be based on how yesterday was. Or is your mind filled with the anxiety of how tomorrow's events will have a negative outcome? Either way, if you're coming from the disappointments of the past or the anxiety of the future, your "come from" will dictate your attitude, the way you show up in life for that day, and the present moment.

Instead, I'm going to teach you how to come from the present moment, and the present possibilities. By being fully present in the moment, you will be in tune to more things available to you, everything that you need at that moment, and you'll never be lacking. See, the secret is, if you're fully present in the conversation, at the moment with the other person, you will not need anything outside of that moment.

You have a confidence, a peace, which grounds you. To be fully available, fully there at that moment, there's nothing else needed, and your come from is at the present moment of what's available. Not only what is available, but also what is missing for this moment to get the intended results that you're committed to. Then the fun begins when you get to create what is missing!

Coming from history is coming from a scarcity mentality. There isn't enough, there hasn't ever been enough, I'm not enough. Our conversation is measured based on what we can do. When we work from what we can do, it leads us to what we can have. Now you're going to be depressed for a minute if you follow me through this thought. If you can only have based on what you can do, then you won't have much. Most of us are aware that we are limited in what we can do. Can you be a doctor, lawyer, engineer, teacher, businessperson, etc? Most of us can be one and some of us can be two of these roles and very few can be three or more. So if I can't "do" that much, then I won't ever have that much. Make sense? Now the depressing part. If you can't do that much, therefore you won't have that much, when will you become significant or happy or fulfilled? This is a "doing" conversation: my self worth or significance is based on how much I do, so I can have, then I will become, happy, fulfilled. That is where a scarcity mind set comes from, a doing conversation.

However, if you wake up excited for a new day, you're normally coming from a BE-ing mindset. You're committed to BE-ing what is needed for your goal to be achieved. You're committed to BE-ing a great businessperson, to have what great business people have, and then you will do with what you have. Or you're committed to BE-ing a great spouse and do what great spouses do, and have the relationships great spouses have. The bottom line is you're committed to BE-ing, and from there you're overflowing into what you do and have. Look at this chart and you will see the subtle yet powerful distinction of BE-ing abundant versus scarce.

SCARCITY	**ABUNDANCE**	**ABUNDANCE**
Do	**Be**	**Be**
Have	Do	Have
Become	Have	Do
Works Significance	**Grace Significance**	**Grace Significance**

Works Significance: Doing something to have something, then you're saved (sense of self worth, significance through having). That is until you see someone else having more then you, then you're back on the treadmill of doing to have, then becoming significant. It doesn't work, therefore its death.

Grace Significance: Grace being free and unmerited favor. If you come from a place that is given to you without strings attached then from that BE-ing, your doing will naturally flow and attract what you have. If you believe you didn't have to earn who you are, then you're under grace. You come from an understanding that you already are, without having to earn the position and then you naturally do from that way of BE-ing. Or from your way of BE-ing, you will naturally have then do with what you have.

It's easier then it sounds. I have four children and my three oldest are boys. They all play sports and there is no way I could go to each of their events, even if that was my full time job. Some sporting events are on the same day and at the same time, it's impossible. So I can't do (go to every game possible) to have (their trust) and then become (a great dad).

Instead, I work from Grace Significance and know that I'm already a great dad and I do what great dads do and have what great dads have. I schedule the boys' final events on my calendar, then I back fill their games, then I communicate with them about which events I won't be able to make and why. That's doing what great dads do! Then I have what great dads have, and that's my boys' understanding, love, and respect.

I didn't grow up with a role model or a dad to teach me this. Then how did I know how to be a great dad and perform from Grace versus Works Significance? I did the opposite of what I would consider a bad dad to do. A bad dad would not communicate, or be intentional in scheduling the final events, and would make excuses of why he missed certain events. I can go on and on. So instead of doing those things, I did the opposite.

Can you see the distinction now? This chapter is about whether you come from a place of abundance or scarcity. When you wake up in the morning, where do you come from? A new possibility of the day, abundance? Do you come from a place of excitement that today offers you unlimited possibilities and that you believe that God, the Universe, luck, or whatever else you believe in, has a plan and a purpose for you? Personally, I believe that the creator of Heaven and Earth, which is God, has a plan for me every morning, and it's a game between both of us, that we get to explore and engage in together while opportunities and possibilities are set before me. Like a little kid, I get to find the possibility waiting for me!

How do you wake up in the morning? What's your "come from?" Is it past failures and you're dragging yourself out of bed hoping today won't be like yesterday because it was so horrible, which is a scarcity mentality? Or is your "come from" missed opportunities from the past, and you're still beating yourself up thinking, "Damn it, I should have done that. Why did I let that person go? What a stupid decision I made!" And you're beating yourself up. Or is your "come from" when you wake, "Man, there's no way I'll be able to reproduce that success. Nothing can be better than that past victory." Where's your "come from?" See, your "come from" is so significant and sets the tone of everything you do that day and have currently.

Waking up before the alarm clock goes off, my natural tendency is to go back to sleep until the alarm clock wakes me up. Instead, I remind myself of my WHY question! (I'll teach you how to find your WHY in the coming chapters.)

"Who do I get to inspire today to take action by connecting to their WHY?"

Then a surge of energy goes through my body. My "come from" is not, "please just 30 more minutes of sleep. I'm so tired" or "yesterday was so tough, I don't want to face what today is going to bring me." Or "I don't know what today will bring me." Those "come from" thoughts are based on eating crumbs off the table versus setting the table. When your "come from" is anchored in your WHY, you get to set the table. You get to create the day to move toward your WHY. I get to inspire a leader today to be what she or he longs to BE. I get to take charge of my life and set the table and eat what I choose and not the crumbs off the floor that life gives me.

Let's go set the table!

CHAPTER 2

You Are In

"Remember, you have been criticizing yourself for years and it hasn't worked. Try approving of yourself and see what happens."

Louise L. Hay

About second grade, I remember this new game we played when we went out for recess one day. The kids said, "Hey Sabastian, got this new game. You ready to play?" I was like, "Yeah, of course!" These are my best friends, I grew up with them, I saw them on a daily basis. Out of nowhere, they made this horseshoe around me. I looked to my left, to my right, looked behind me, no one else is on my team. I'm standing there by myself and all of a sudden the kids, out of nowhere, begin saying things I never heard come out of their mouth before. They used their fingers, pulling their eyes back and start calling me chink, gook, china man and some names I didn't even recognize. I didn't even know what they were saying at the time, I just knew I was the butt of the joke. I knew it was them versus me. They started running backwards and as they were running backwards, that was my cue to chase them as they called me these names that I was not familiar with, and by the tone they were saying it, didn't sound encouraging. It was very hateful. It was very belittling.

I remember from that day forward, I never wanted to hear those words again, that you're not like us. See, that's what a scarcity mentality looks like. A scarcity mentality looks like there's not enough and the children that day were dichotomizing who they were and who I was. They were better then me, they were the dominant culture and I was the lesser. Yes, it was in the mid-70s during the Vietnam War. There was a tension in America and I'm sure their parents taught them how to be discriminate.

When I came to America in early 70's with an American stepfather, I was only 4 years old. I grew up thinking I was Caucasian. I was an American. I was white. I was going to Catholic school and grew up with these kids since I can remember. I had the same stepfather as long as I can remember. So for them to say I was not like them was devastating. It didn't stop there. They took it to the next level and said that my "father" wasn't my father. What? This was the only "father" I knew. Who is he then? Who am I? I was devastated and committed to never being different again so that I wouldn't hear that painful phrase, "you're not like us."

What a scarcity mentality does, it segregates, it separates and those kids' parents couldn't tell the difference from a North Vietnamese person versus a South Vietnamese person, much less someone who was Chinese, someone who was Korean, or someone who was Japanese. They just saw Asians being the same and who where a threat to their way of life.

I have a completely different understanding now as an adult but as a child, I saw it as me not having enough – a scarcity mentality. I wasn't part of the "in" group, society, or dominate culture. I wasn't accepted. Instead, I needed to preform for acceptance.

When we were in fifth grade, my best friend Kenny and I would go to convenience store in the morning and empty our pockets of coins we collected from day before. We counted how much we had collectively and then bought our breakfast. Regardless of how much money we had, whatever we bought, we shared it with excitement and joy! Sometimes we only had enough for a single honey bun, no chocolate milk, nothing else. Just a single honey bun and for some reason it was always the best honey bun.

It was never about how much money we had or who brought how much. It was always about our contribution to one another and sharing the results of what we brought that morning.

Abundance isn't about quantity, it's about contribution. Knowing your differences, distinctions, and odd quirks are uniquely yours. That is what makes you abundant. Knowing you have yourself to offer and that is more then enough. There is nothing to prove, or more you need. Your contribution to the conversation, to the project, to the event, to the relationship is exactly what is needed. Nothing more, nothing less, just you "BEING" fully present.

To live out this abundant mindset, you have to know you're already In, accepted. You see, if I looked at it from an abundant mindset, even at the young age of being a second grader, I could have seen that the kids who mocked me were really saying, you're uniquely and wonderfully created. There is no one else that could be just like you, Sabastian. From that, I would have seen myself as a contribution to the community. I could have seen myself as someone who has something to offer, who is already accepted and approved and didn't have to perform for acceptance, and didn't have to compromise my identity to adapt to theirs.

See, abundance already knows you're accepted and you're approved. You are already in. I was already accepted before I was playing the game. I was already on the playground, running around, chasing them or being chased by them. I didn't have to perform. So, when you're already in, there's a confidence within you. There is a burning urgency to give yourself away because you know you can make value and create possibilities for yourself and other people.

Even in second grade, if I had been taught what I'm teaching you (what you can teach the next generation, what you can teach your clients), I could have had an abundance mindset. You have to have an abundant mindset. You have to know that you're already in. You have to believe that you're already a contributor to the story that we're part of, to this universe that we get an impact and improve. You have to believe that you're already in. When you believe that, then new possibilities and opportunities open up for you in ways you couldn't have seen from a scarce mentality.

So, it starts off now with you believing that you're already in. You don't have to perform. You don't have to compare. You don't have to look for approval. But, what would it look like if every day you came from a place of already being approved? You wake up to know that you don't have to perform. You get to provide. You get to provide what is missing in this universe. You get to provide what's missing in your relationships. You get to provide what's missing in your career. You get to provide for yourself and others because you're already complete and whole.

What would it look like if you came from a place of wholeness that you already are a great father so you do what great fathers do? Then you have what great fathers have, and you get to enjoy what great fathers enjoy. What if you're already great businesswomen? What if you're already a great coach? If you were a great coach, you get to have what great coaches have, then you get to do with what you have. You don't have to perform, you're already there instead of performing. You're providing. You're providing for your clients. You're providing for whatever's needed and wanted in the moment because you're abundant. You're more than enough and you're part of the solution.

You're in because there is no one else like you! And all your differences, uniqueness and self-identified quirks are what make you, well you! So add to the story of life, bring more color to each conversation without having to compare, perform or conform. You're in, show up and confidently be what's missing!

Finally, I believe you don't have to perform for acceptance, you're already in this amazing story we call life. Look at the evidence, you're here, you're reading this book. You want to transform other peoples' lives by being this amazing coach. The Creator of Heaven and Earth accept you already. In fact, my belief is the Creator did not only accept you, but created you to be a contribution to this story were living in. Your unquiet difference, the quirks you have, the imperfection, fears, emotions, attitude, experiences - everything about you is to be what is missing in our daily conversations, actions, and events that make this world so great.

You're not an accident, you didn't somehow enter this story from a back door and need to fit in and perform for acceptance. You are to show up boldly and uniquely you! Bring that version of yourself to the coaching conversation and see magic happen. See your clients become more confident in themselves because you are confident in yourself. Remember you're the container in which your client will expand from. The more you're vulnerable, transparent and unique, the more your client has the space to be those things.

I think one of the major mistakes of temperament assessments or personality tests are they are not clearer on stating that the results of the assessments or test are only a base line of your similarities to the human race. In no way should anyone walk away from these assessments and test thinking they are in a box and like everyone else. I am a huge DISC assessment champion. In fact, I am a master trainer and coach for the DISC assessment and have done DISC Sales, DISC Leadership, and DISC Relationship training. DISC is only a tool to give us a springboard of common language to discover our uniqueness based on the intensity and degree of our temperaments, and never is it to be used to pigeon hole, corner, or put anyone in a box.

Jump into the story of life, bring your unique self and add to each chapter of life what is missing! Show up and make life more colorful, exciting, and worth exploring! You're In, don't perform for acceptance, show up with your one-of-a-kind uniqueness and change the world!

CHAPTER 3

You Can

"The worst loneliness is to not be comfortable with yourself."

Mark Twain

In the previous chapter, we talked about that you're already in. No longer do you have to perform, you're already accepted. It's not based on what I'm saying. It's the mere reality that you're in this world. Look around. You're already in the story line of this world regardless if you believe in a Creator, a God, The Universe, karma, or Buddha. Whatever you may believe the truth is, you're here. You're reading this book. You're alive. You're part of the human race. You're already In. If you're already in, then in this chapter you will realize you Can. That's right, you Can. You can do the desires of your heart. You can be what no one else is. In fact, it's not that you have the ability to, you have to - because if you don't become the masterpiece that you're created to be, then you're going to miss out on this life that only you can live. You Can.

See, the reason some people want to be musicians, others want to be doctors, others want to be engineers, others want to be entrepreneurs, others ones want to be a coach, it's because there's that desire in their heart that shows you their uniqueness. Now even all of us, and if you're reading this book hopefully you want to be a successful six-figure coach, it's life changing personally and it changes other people's lives. It impacts whole societies, communities and the world. If all of us want to be coaches does that mean we're all exactly the same? In fact, I'd argue with you none of us are the same. We may have the same skeleton and same blueprints, but our flesh that makes us uniquely different are different. That's why I'm encouraging you that you can be the desire on your heart.

No longer do you have to live in fear that you can't be like someone else because you don't have to compare yourself to others. There's no comparison. You're already in the story. You don't have to compete and perform to be in the story.

If you're already in the story you can be what you want to be, the character that you're called to be in the story line. You don't have to compare yourself to anyone else. See, that's abundance. When you don't have to compare yourself to anyone else, that means there's more than enough for everyone. No longer you're competing or comparing, but you can be fully you, uniquely different and that's what it's all about. If you're not uniquely different, then you're just the same as everyone else and if you're the same as everyone else, then you can't be you. Then you will be a cheaper version of someone else - an imitation, a fake, simply a knock off. If you can't be an original, masterpiece, unique version of yourself, then you won't produce the results you needed to be a six-figure coach.

There's a longing in you. How do I know? You bought the book. You desire and long for a lifestyle that allows you to be fully you, flexible, coach from anywhere, travel, have time with your family, not just time, quality time with your family and enjoy your life because you're making an impact in other people's lives and the world.

Let me dive deeper into my story that I opened up with earlier. As a second grader, being ridiculed, racially discriminated against, and belittled. Not for anything I did, just for my mere existence as a human being. I was different. I didn't know I was already In. I thought I was less than, and I had to perform for acceptance, so I'd never ever again hear those words, "You're not like us." Those words, "You're not like us" came from a place of scarcity. From that place of emptiness, I asked myself, "What would it take for me to be like you?" I performed, I mimicked, I was a hypocrite, and I acted any way needed for people to accept me to be just like them versus being truly me.

See, this chapter, once you get past the scarce mentality, there is not enough, I'm not enough. Then you get into abundance mindset, I'm enough, there is enough in this world for everyone. When people say you're not like us, it's no longer a negative connotation. It's praise. It's an acknowledgement. It's an invitation for you being exactly who you are so you don't have to pretend to be anyone else. In this chapter, You Can. You Can do those things that are on your heart, those passions, those desires, because you no longer have to compare yourself to anyone else because you're not like them. You're not like me. You're not like anyone. You're uniquely and wonderfully created. You are so different that the mere fact that you try to be like anyone else is a travesty, it's a loss, and it's an insult you and the Creator who made you. You are created uniquely and distinctly different so that you can be a contribution and enhance all the possibilities of this universe. To enhance conversations. To enhance relationships. To enhance how wonderful and beautiful this world is.

You have to know you can. The reason that passion is on your heart is because you are uniquely and wonderful created to do it. Yes you, that is why you saw it, "You spot it, you got it." There's no more comparison. You have all this desire to be coaches and you are reading this book because you want to be a six-figure coach. You want to learn the way of BE-ing so that you can command a six-figure income, because you know you can provide value for your clients, and you can live a lifestyle, that's the passion on your heart, so you have freedom and flexibility.

Right now, I'm on vacation with my family writing this chapter. I don't have to be secluded to a certain environment or lifestyle. I have freedom because I can. It's a passion in my heart to be able to travel with my family and experience this beautiful world and the diversity of people and not be locked down in one location. I Can. You Can. There's no more comparison about how things need to be done or if you're doing it right. If you want to compare yourself to anyone else, compare yourself to yourself. Every day are you a better version of yourself? Every day, love more than you loved yesterday. Every day, forgive more than you forgave yesterday. Every day, create more value for others than you did yesterday. If you want to compare yourself, compare yourself to what you were doing yesterday, and make an incremental improvement today.

Second, the reason You Can is because you'll do it different than anyone else. Being unique is this. You are free from comparison because what you do will be uniquely done that day. It will be unprecedented. No one else has ever done it the way you have done it. You see, as coaches, I'm going to give you the framework. I'm going to give you the step-by-step how to be a six-figure coach. That will give you a foundational coaching technique or model before you start coaching people from your way of BE-ing to get them results.

Even though I give you this framework, it's like a skeleton. You've got to put the flesh on it. You will do it different from me and everyone else because your character, your life history, your personality, your experiences, your joys, your pain, everything you brought into life up until this moment will put the flesh on the skeleton on the coaching model. It's going to be different. You have to embrace that. That's okay. In fact, it's not just okay, it's what's needed, what's wanted in this world. Your flavor, your style, your personality.

If I could teach my four children anything in this world, it's not to compare themselves. They're unique and wonderfully created. Just say, for example, all four of my children want to be a doctor. Guess what? There are many different types of doctors they can be. They can work in the laboratory and do research, be a traditional family doctor, or they can be a specialist, like a neurosurgeon. There's a myriad of doctors out there, and let's just say all four of them want to be an exact same neurosurgeon. Like I said, being a neurosurgeon is just a skeleton. The framework. They'll all bring their own personality, experiences, and temperament into being that neurosurgeon. They'll influence the nurses, patients and the hospital in a different way. They'll all make different levels of income, as long as they stay uniquely different.

Let me get back to my story. I had to find out the hard way, but I had this passion in my heart for coaching. I have to admit, I was never trained by a six-figure coach. I stumbled and fumbled my way forward because I knew this is what I want to do. This is what I was passionate about. I became that six-figure coach because I knew I could. It was a painful journey.

During elementary school, my parents got divorced. I moved from one state where my stepfather was living to another state with my mom. The most painful part about the divorce was losing the only male role model I had. I didn't realize I was always "IN" (that I was already accepted and approved) and I didn't have to perform for others to appreciate or like me. If you've done any research or you know anything about psychology and the need for a male influence in a young man's life, that last insult devastated me. I didn't have a male role model. I was questioning who my stepfather was, why he wasn't by biological father. I always thought he was my biological father. Has he been lying to me? Who was my biological father? This was traumatic for me.

Then, I carried this echo in the back of my head (the kids' saying you're not like us, you're not like us) and I never wanted to hear those words again, and wanted to perform for everyone's acceptance. We moved to this big city where the very first time I saw someone else who was not like me. See, the kids back in my hometown, the little Catholic school I attended, they were all Caucasian. My mother, sister, myself were the only ones who were not Caucasians. I thought the kids were making fun of me because I had a better tan than they did. Well, the truth was, they were making fun of me because they didn't know how to celebrate my difference.

I took that as a scarce mentality and moved into a big city with my sister and mom. Then for the first time, I saw somebody else with a better tan than I did. I stared at that person. I was mesmerized. Wow, not only does that person have a better tan than me, but there was something wrong with that person. Their eyes are not like mine. Their eyes were rounder. Did you notice that? Did you notice how in a scarce mentality everything's about comparing? I couldn't celebrate that person's uniqueness or difference, I was comparing them to myself. Did you notice how I couldn't appreciate their tan being better than mine? I felt insecure and I had to criticize their tan. Then, it didn't stop there, I had to magnify their differences and elevate my significance by noticing that their eyes are not like mine. Their eyes are too round. That person who had a better tan than I did, I learned that person was called a Mexican. I saw a Mexican for the very first time in my life and it kind of devastated me. I didn't know what to do with it. I was in that scarce mentality. I was in that comparison mode. There wasn't enough.

Well then, soon after, not only did I see somebody that had a better tan than I did, I believed I saw the person with the most ultimate tan. A tan I could never achieve. Yes, I saw a black person for the very first time and I said, "Oh my, this person has an ultimate tan," but wait, I couldn't celebrate that. I had to compare. I said, "Well they might have a better tan than me, but there's something wrong with their body." They're too big and muscular and athletic. All these positive qualities, but I had to make them negative because I was in this comparison mode. Because I didn't know at that time I can yet. I can be unique, I can be passionate, and I can have a value system different from other people. That journey of finding that I can be uniquely different from them, in fact, I am uniquely different from them, didn't kick in until later.

Besides my mom and my sister, I saw the very first other Asian I had ever seen. Boy, did I have a field day pulling that person apart! Not only did I compare their tan to mine, but I compared their hair, their eyes, and their body structure. I just picked and pulled them apart as much as possible to degrade them, to minimize them so I could elevate myself, out of my insecurity, out of my scarcity. To BE a six-figure coach, accept the principle that you're already in, you're accepted, you're approved, and you CAN. You don't have to compare.

Until you really understand these principles, it will be difficult for you to have consistency in BE-ing a six-figure coach. You can do the desires on your heart because you're uniquely and wonderfully different. I was different from the Mexican kids I grew up with. I was different from the black kids I grew up with. I was different from the Caucasian kids I grew up with. I was different from the Asian kids I grew up with. Until I accepted that, I didn't have the freedom to be unique. I tried to mimic the Mexican kids, the African-American kids, the Caucasian kids. Even the Asian kids, I tried to mimic. I didn't have success with any people group because I wasn't any one of those. I grew up in the Caucasian culture being a minority. I grew up in a Latino culture being a minority. I grew up with black culture as a minority. Then with Asians, I was still a minority, because I was not really Asian.

Through all that pain, it did propel me to accept myself being uniquely different. Until I could accept myself being uniquely different, I wasn't able to chase my passion, my dream, to be where I'm at today, making over six-figures a year as a coach. Becoming a business consultant. Working with companies three to five years at a time, because I could continue creating value for them, and still have the flexible lifestyle I want without being tied down to a traditional nine-to-five job. My values are different from most because I know I can. I know I'm living in an abundant world, there's more than enough. That I don't have to conform or compare myself to other people and their results, but I get to create my own results because I can.

CHAPTER 4

You Count

Honesty is a very expensive gift, don't expect it from cheap people.

Warren Buffett

You Count, your feedback into other people's life matters. See, people will live life to the best of their ability and in this abundant mindset there's more for them. The universe, God, wants to give them more than they have that's why it's called abundant mindset. If you believe that, then your every interaction with clients counts because your job as a coach is to speak into their life in such a way that they become the biggest version of themselves. They become exactly what they want to be for their goal and dreams. Without you speaking into their life, without you giving them feedback, how will they know if they're on-track or off-track of being the greatest version of themselves in that moment? In fact, you'd literally be robbing them if you didn't speak into their life and give them feedback. They would not see the fullest potential they could be in the moment, in their vision, and to the world!

They wouldn't see life in HD if you held back and didn't give them feedback. You count. Without you, things taste a little bit less because you didn't bring your unique self, the needed seasoning in their life. What we talked about in the last chapter that you can. When you don't show them the fullness of who you are and uniqueness of who you are, you rob a little bit from the person and the people you're with because they don't get to see the fullness of that moment. What creates fullness in that moment is your contribution into the conversation, into the issue, into the celebration. Whatever it may be, if you don't fully show up and your contribution is not experienced by others and you're not giving feedback, then the moment is less than and literally you're robbing people of that moment

You Count. Your contribution, your participation enhances the experience of each person, community, and the world. Without you, it'd be less. It's like drinking a flat soda. Yeah, I can drink it, I can taste the sugar content, but it's flat. You bring the enhanced flavor and take the conversation or relationship to the next level. You count.

As I continue my story of growing up and growing out of the scarce mentality into the abundant mentality, this story I'm about to share sounds far-fetched. Most of you who are reading this may not be able to connect really right away, or maybe at all. I hope you can pull out the principles from this story and understand. I wanted to keep it raw and authentic so you could completely see the transformation for me from a scarce mentality to abundant mentality. See in this chapter that you count! The most beautiful part is you know you have a contribution to this world. You know you have a contribution to in every interaction you have today. You know you have a contribution to this universe, this planet, this nature - the animals, the plants and this whole world. You're such a contribution.

How do you know? Because evidence reveals, the fact that you woke up this morning, the fact that you're reading this book right now shows that you count. The evidences shows you are invited to participate in this grand story of life and to bring your uniqueness. Let me show you what your contribution looks like when I say, "You Count." We count in many different ways, but specifically for a coach what makes you count is the fact that you can give feedback. Now, we can go into a whole chapter on feedback, but at this point, you have to understand feedback is neutral. It's not positive or negative. It's not constructive criticism. It's speaking into the gap of what's missing.

You can't speak into the gap of what's missing unless you understand someone's vision and their current reality. What's the gap between their current reality and their vision? That's where you get to speak into and give feedback. Here's the most beautiful part when you give feedback to your clients, to your relationships, to total strangers, you'll see how much you count. But first you need to know their vision, their current reality and be able to speak into their gap. You'll see how much value you create. You'll see how much this world is missing your presence if you don't show up.

Let me give you an example from my story. I told you I grew up with an American stepfather in a predominantly

Caucasian community. Got racially discriminated against as a little child in second grade. Didn't know my identity and I was conforming to find it. Finding other people had a better tan than myself. Then realizing that I'm uniquely different from them. I'm still on this journey. I haven't fully realized I can yet. That's okay being uniquely different. I'm flirting with it. I'm experimenting. I'm seeing where it's safe and letting it out slowly. Maybe you can relate. There're certain safe places that we can be a fool and not be criticized for it. We'll test those places and be a bigger fool, make funnier jokes, or bomb on our jokes, but we try to joke around more in those venues.

For me, it was growing with a community, actually a family of Latinos. I grew up with a lot low-income Mexicans. I didn't know at the time, I thought it was just normal life, but the kids I grew up with had uncles and fathers, who were second and third generation, bringing drugs across the border from Mexico. As they brought it over, the drugs would be in these duffle bags. I'd watch them open the bags. I was probably in sixth grade at the time, very young. They'd open the bags, and I'd see them take out some white stuff, cut it up, and measure it, blah, blah, blah. Then I'd see them take out some green plants, and cut it up and put it in these bags.

One day I was looking and they're cutting up marijuana, putting them in the bags, getting ready for distribution . . . this is a little sixth-grader here . . . I looked at what they were doing and I said, "Hey Uncle, have you ever considered doing X, Y, and Z? Maybe you can get more of each cut. They said, "What? We have been doing this for generations. Chino, who are you to tell us how to cut this up? You're just a kid." I said, "Well, I'm sorry. I didn't mean to insult you. I was just watching and I noticed, just something clicked in my head if you would have done X, Y, and Z, you would probably get more."

They all started laughing and chuckling, and they go, "We like that. We like that you're ambitious. We like that you think you know what you're doing, so what we're going do," . . . remember I'm a sixth grader . . . "What we're going to do is give you a quarter bag." I had no idea what a quarter bag was. I was just excited they were going to give me something because they believed in me. "And then you get to go sell it.

If you think you're so great go sell it. If you can sell all this in a week, and come back, and you have some money left over we'll sell you more."

That was my little journey as my first entrepreneur business adventure. See, I spoke to what was missing for them. I saw their vision. They wanted to make income. I saw their current reality. I saw them get the raw material and their production line to make the final product. I saw there's something missing. I spoke into that gap, not only to create value for myself, but by them trusting me and giving me my first product to sell, I created value for them. I was their loyal customer. I started coming back and buying more and more from them. See, even though that was a negative context, that was my first memory that I counted, that my feedback in speaking to the gap, to speak what was missing, not only created value for myself but for them.

Now as a coach, I know I count because I'm fully present with my clients. I'm out of my scarcity mentality and I'm in the abundance mentality. I don't have to compare myself with another coach. I have the freedom to be uniquely me to speak into their gap and create value for them. The key is for me to count. I need to know their vision. What are they committed to? Where are they going? I need to see the current reality. Where are they kind of stuck? What's missing from them that I can speak into that gap?

Here's the funniest part, most of the time when I speak into the gap they already know it. Not only did they know their own gap, many other people knew about it too. What I find is I'm the only one with the courage, with the commitment and the confidence to speak into the gap, to create value for them. You notice that? When I count, when I believe that I count, that I contribute, I fill in that gap. Without me, there would be a lack in the conversation, and lack in the relationship. I'm the missing piece of the puzzle to that relationship, to that conversation.

When I believe that, I come in and speak into the gap that no one else dares to speak into because they're still scarce. They don't think they can. They don't think they count. Since I do believe that I'm already in, I can and I count, I get to create value for other people. I can become what is missing. I can speak into the gap and I can create value.

That's the foundation. Those are your three principles that will make you a six-figure coach. That is the demarcation. That is why most people can never break the six-figure mark in coaching because they don't have the way of being. It's not the sexy systematic coaching tool or process, which I will offer you later. The accountability coaching system I've been using has made me six figures and over year after year. I can give you that process right now. I can give you that accountability-coaching model right now.

Unless you have these three principles of (1) You Are In, (2) You Can, and (3) You Count, most likely you will not be able to make six figures. If you are lucky to do it in one year and you will not be able to reproduce it, because it starts off right here – that being a six-figure coach requires a foundation of abundance. You have to have that foundational stance of abundance. When your cup overflows, that's when you start making six figures. That's when you start creating value. That's when you exceed the expectation of your client because You Are In, You Can and You Count. Those three fundamental principles are the foundation of any coaching model and particularly for the one I'll teach you how to make six figures.

Summarizing what you have read up till now.

These beginning chapters focus on your way of BE-ing. Remember an abundance mentality starts off with you BE-ing and from your BE-ing, you do and then have. Or from your way of BE-ing, you have, then do with what you have. Regardless, you always start off from BE-ing.

Scarce Mentality	**Abundant Mentality**	**Abundant Mentality**
Do	**BE**	**BE**
Have	Do	Have
Become	Have	Do

From this abundant mindset, we know we are already In. We are in the story of life. We no long have to perform for acceptance. We perform out of acceptance! That is a totally different energy!

We know if we are already In, then we Can. We Can be unique and different. We don't need to compare or conform to others. We don't need to paint inside someone else's lines. We're not limited by traditional process or procedures. We Can be uniquely us and uniquely different.

Finally, from an abundant mindset, we know we're already In, we Can be uniquely different, then what we do counts, we Count! I remember the movie titled, "A day without Mexicans." You don't have to watch the movie to get the point. Here in Southern California, Mexico is our neighbor and immigrants do the majority of low labor jobs from Mexico. We know what a day without Mexicans would be like, a very difficult day.

That's the same with you and me. What would a day be like without you or me? I know my children would miss me, my wife wouldn't have anyone making her coffee in the mornings, and my clients wouldn't have someone champion their vision. The world would be different, "less-than," without me showing up fully.

Now that we have established these foundational principles of BE-ing a six-figure coach, let me give you the foundational coaching model to move any client from point A to point B.

CHAPTER 5

Your Why

"The purpose of life is not to be happy. It is to be useful, to be honorable, to be compassionate, to have it make some difference that you have lived and lived well."

Ralph Waldo Emerson

Marcus wanted to increase his client list by 20%. John wanted to start his speaking career. Jennifer wanted a promotion. Sonny wanted to add extra 25% revenue in his department. I told each of these clients I couldn't create results for them until they told me their Why. Each of them looked at me as if I was crazy. I was to create results with them as a coach and I'm slowing them down by asking them their Why? Because that was the next step in their career, keeping their business afloat, or next logical step for them to stay competitive.

I don't disagree with any of those statements; I just can't accept them for their face value. I need to know the drivers behind these goals. I need to know the source they are coming from. I need to know their purpose, motivation, their Why.

Most people think our Why comes from our passion, our ambition, the natural trajectory of our life based on our parent's upbringing, the environment we grew up in, the educational system. It's almost like this directed path that we're guided towards equals our purpose. The truth is many people have these false starts. Many entrepreneurs start something and they reach the top and they collapse or implode. Many leaders and entrepreneurs launch in a direction, they quit and they turn, launch another direction, quit and turn again. Do you ever wonder why your purpose never seems like it's your purpose? How do you find your purpose? Well, I use the word "purpose" interchangeably with Why for you to connect with it for a moment.

Do you ever question why you start things and quit? Why you're not constantly excited and motivated by something? Well, because I believe your purpose or you're Why comes from a different source. It's counterintuitive. I don't think you can find many books or articles on this. I found this on my own personal journey and validated by hundreds and hundreds of people I've coached. I call it the stand. What's your stand? What are you committed to creating and being responsible for?

Earlier I told you my stand as a coach is to inspire leaders to take action by connecting to their Why. I could say that confidently and boldly. When I chose the word "I inspire," I wrestled with the word. Is it professional enough? I get people results, should I have used that word? If I chose to use results, then I would have started sounding like everyone else. I wasn't living out the other principle that I can be different and unique. I started asking my past clients, "What did I create for you? What value do I create for you now? What would make you hire me again?" They said, "Sabastian, you inspire me to get my goal."

At first, I took an offense to that. What about the results I got you when you lost 20 pounds in 10 weeks? What about when you got 15% month over month increased on your department's profits after the initial 10 weeks coaching?

What about those other results I got you when you resolved your conflict with the other departments and now you guys are collaborating and creating more value for your company? Are you telling me I inspired you? I had to sit with that and as I sat with it, I found out I inspire people. I breathe in spirit and I give people life.

What? No, I'm not saying I'm God. Please. I'm saying I inspire, I breathe life into them, give them hope. I motivate them, encourage them to live life, to step into the life that God, the creator of heavens and earth, created for them. I see the best version of them and I invite them into it. I invite them into their dream, goal, and vision. I inspire leaders.

I just don't inspire any person, I inspire leaders. People who influence other people, people who have carried the flag, took up the gauntlet, put on the mantle to say I will lead you and they have chosen to give their life to be the tip of the arrow and go through the pain points of life first. Those are the leaders that I inspire.

I support them take action, because in leadership, as you know, it's weary being the tip of the arrow to penetrating through hard obstacles and resistance and to be focused and hit your target. You get fatigued, beaten up, worn down, and at times, you don't want to take any more action. You settle. You get complacent. See, as a coach, I inspire leaders to take action because that's what leaders do. I remind them that they have to take action, that's what leaders do, that is their WHY. Then other people behind them can take action, to get their goal and vision.

When leaders are not taking action they got disconnected from their Why. I connect them to their Why. I connect them to their purpose, their vision, and their goal. I connect them to something that's deep inside of them that bring out the best of them. I connect them to the emotion that they cannot deny or hide; that gives them all the energy and purpose they need when nothing else gives it to them. It comes intrinsically from within, not from without.

I believe your WHY comes from your pain. Your WHY comes from a place from your history, your past. See, coaching is not for everyone. You have to have certain life experience, certain maturity, mostly certain scars and success before you coach other people. You're not a mentor. You're not a counselor. You're a coach. A coach gets results for others, but first, they have to have results for themselves. If you don't understand how to get people to their WHY, they won't take action because their Why is from within, not from without.

The Why comes from a place that can generate energy, passion, and action, just simply, because they got connected to it? It's an emotion and an energy source that comes from their history, and specifically from their past pain.

There are three periods of human development. If you look into these three periods and find your pain in each stage or period, you'll find your WHY. The first period is called the imprint. That's from zero, from birth to age seven. We're like sponges absorbing everything around us. That's your imprint stage. Then, the next stage is your modeling period. That's from 8 to 13. We're copycats from others influence on us. We copy teachers, older siblings, leaders and parents. The last stage is our socialization stage. Between the age 13 and 21, we're really influenced by our peers' acceptance. We develop our character and our self-esteem based on our peers. We look for evidence of those peers to support who we think we need to be.

In those three stages if you see the pain of what I call your significant emotional event, S.E.E. If you could see your significant emotional event, S.E.E., that happened to you, and you'll see a thread that makes up your WHY. For me, from zero to seven the only thing I could remember was a time where at school, and I was the only minority and all the Caucasian kids came up with a game and basically rejected me. In that rejection, I told myself I would never be rejected again. I would be accepted and approved by the majority. Then during my modeling period when I started copying everybody, leaders and teachers and parents, I started to become a people pleaser. I started doing whatever they wanted me to do or need me to do so I wouldn't hear those words "rejection" again.

Then finally, when I got to 14 years old through 21 years of age, to validate my significance and my importance, and that I'm accepted and socially acceptable, I found peers who would validate me. I took leadership and rebelled again the norm that rejected me. I took risks. I led them. People who wanted to go to the next level influenced me. If I would take the risk, they would follow and I would be significant. In those three stages of being rejected from a group of dominant culture, then conforming to the dominant culture so I wouldn't be rejected again, and then finally leading a culture of minorities to make up our own culture and become the dominant culture by rebelling again the status quo, I found my Why, my purpose.

I'm a reluctant coach. I'm a reluctant leader. I'm a reluctant husband, a reluctant father. I didn't want to be where I'm at today. The pressure to do and do more so that I can have more and then finally one day I would become significant was too overwhelming. As you learned in the very opening chapters, the abundant mind says, "I'm already In. I'm already a great coach. I do what great coaches do and I have the results that great coaches have. I'm a great father. I do what great fathers do and I get the results that great fathers have. I am a great husband. I have what great husbands have, then I do with what I have, that great husbands do."

When I come from an abundant mindset, I'm no longer a reluctant coach, a reluctant husband, a reluctant father, a reluctant friend, a reluctant leader. I'm a proud, confident and bold coach because I found my Why. My Why comes from my pain of rejection and lack of acceptance. Now I am the leader who teaches people how to be accepted, how to get results, that proves their passion and purpose. No longer am I reluctant. I'm confident, borderline arrogant, because I come from a place that I'm already approved and accepted, and because I come from that place, my Why is to teach people to be approved and accepted.

Your Why doesn't come from ambition. That only lasts so long. Your Why comes from a place of your pain. Your pain shapes your "come from." If you could accept it, you'll find that your pain, the significant emotional events (S.E.E.) you had through those three periods of imprint, modeling, socialization, is giving you an invitation for a purpose that will generate energy when circumstances won't, will generate passion when everyone else is lacking it, will generate a smile when everyone else is frowning, because it's not impacted by what's outside of us. It comes from what's inside of us.

Let's find your Why

STEP ONE

- Set aside 15-30 minutes of uninterrupted time

STEP TWO

- Recall the first "painful" memory you have from the three stages of human development. Don't over think this, there is no right or wrong. Trust yourself and write down the first memory you have from each stage. You can go back later and elaborate or adjust, for now, allow yourself to accept the first memory and write them down for each stage.
- Don't justify the "pain" or S.E.E. Be objective and write it down.
- Don't minimize your S.E.E. because you're now in a different place, allow the S.E.E. to come out as it does, no filters.

STEP THREE

Write down our first memory of any S.E.E. during these stages.

- ***Imprint Stage 0yrs-7yrs***

  _____

  _____

  _____

- ***Modeling Stage 8yrs-13yrs***

  _____

  _____

  _____

- ***Socialization Stage 14yrs-21yrs.***

  _____

  _____

STEP FOUR

- Find the common theme that ties the three S.E.E. together.
- The common theme is usually the opposite of the S.E.E.

Example:

- Imprint Stage 0yrs-7yrs: Parents divorced
- Modeling Stage 8yrs-13yrs: Didn't fit in school
- Socialization Stage 14yrs-21yrs. : Socially isolated
  - Theme: Rejection
  - Why could be driven by
    - Acceptance
    - Inclusiveness
    - Community
  - Why can show up through
    - Adopting children
    - Being a Trainer, Coach, Consultant
    - Building a business to hire and include others

- Inclusive of others, even unhealthy people, into your community, hobbies, and business

As you will see, my client's original request for coaching were driven by a deeper "pain" and only masked by these short term goals. After finding their Why, I ask for a personal and professional goal for the coaching journey.

Coaching Goals	**Personal Goal**	**S.E.E.**	**WHY**
Jeff wanted to add extra 25% revenue in his department.	Run his first marathon	Family had history of health issues	Wanted to be healthy to see his children get married
John wanted to start his speaking career.	Weekly date night with his wife	Grew up without a voice, didn't feel heard	Wanted to share with others that they can have a voice

Coaching Goals	Personal Goal	S.E.E.	WHY
Jennifer wanted a promotion	Get back to her creative hobbies and paint again	She didn't feel seen when around male authority figures	Wanted to know she counted and was just as equal as men are
Mark wanted to increase his client list by 20%.	Lose 15lbs	Grew up overweight and overlooked by other because of his weight	To receive acknowledgement of his work and achievements

Chapter 6

Your Comfort Zone

"The most dangerous person is a bored one"
Sabastian Huynh

A man came upon a construction site where three people were working. He asked the first, "What are you doing?" and the man replied: "I am laying bricks." He asked the second, "What are you doing?" and the man replied: "I am building a wall." As he approached the third, he heard him humming a tune as he worked, and asked, "What are you doing?" The man stood, looked up at the sky, and smiled, "I am building a cathedral!"

This famous story has many principles we can pull from it and it never gets old. I want to highlight how it exposes a person's "come from." Remember your "come from" is your stand. It's where you draw your world view from, where your emotional intelligence was shaped and if you're doing, to have, then become. Or are you BE-ing, and from your BE-ing you do and have. Your "come from' identifies if you have an abundant or scarce mindset.

Let's take a quick look at these three men in the story and see if you can identify their "come from." Remember, all three men are doing the exact same thing, it's their view of what they are doing that is different. The first worker was laying bricks. The second worker is building a wall. The third worker is building a cathedral.

The first two workers are working from of their comfort zone, what they can control. The third is working out of his WHY, what we learned in the past chapter. Let's look at the difference of working out of your comfort zone versus out of your WHY. The importance of understanding this will determine if you can be a six-figure coach.

The comfort zone is simply the space you can control, and you mask it with activities. There are several major spaces you can control: physical, mental, emotional, spiritual, career, health, education, relational and the list can go on and on.

Let me know if this sounds familiar. You wake up in the morning, get the family out the door, fight traffic to work, put in a eight to ten hour day at the office, occasionally go to the gym after work to let the traffic die down. After arriving home, you spend some time with your spouse or children, have dinner, and depending on the night, you might have dinner with friends or just drinks to catch up. You rise and repeat till the weekend. The weekend comes and you sneak some personal time in early Saturday morning. The afternoon is spent with the family doing some kind of activity, then the evening is spent with your extended family or close friends. Sunday morning comes and you're deciding if you want to attend church or sleep in. Regardless what you do, the day flies by and it's already dinner time and you're wondering what did you do all day? After dinner you seem to lose energy thinking about going through the same process again as last week with only a few minor activity changes.

I got depressed writing that! This is the "come from" of the first two construction workers. They spend their life looking at activities to get through the day with. One has a very small perspective of his life and only lays bricks. The second construction worker has a slightly bigger view of his life and is making a wall. Both are in their comfort zone. Here are a couple expressions you might be familiar with so you can see the comfort zone and it's "come from."

When you're in your comfort zone, you play to not lose instead of playing to win. You don't give a 100% because that is risky. You do just enough to get buy. In school you make a 70, that's a "C" and enough so you don't get flunk. At work you fly under the radar and only do what is expected of you and you barely do that well. In relationships you have no expectations, so you're not disappointed or don't disappoint others. You show up only to receive and don't bring anything into the relationship to give. If you did bring something to give to the relationship there is a possibility of rejection, so you stay in your comfort zone, the area of the relationship you can control.

Let me drive this deeper and make us both more depressed. In your health, you don't over eat, avoid most fast foods and watch your calorie intake. You do just enough, but you don't intentionally stick to a diet or life style habit. Last one, I can't type anymore, I'm seriously losing energy and motivation. What does playing not to lose look like in your spiritual life? For some its attending their parents' church four times a year; mother's day, Christmas, Easter and occasionally funerals. Regardless of the religion you practice, you only respond to its traditions and practices when it is convenient for you, ouch!

The reason we play not to lose instead of playing to win is because it is risky for us to show up in life and participate. Participation is dangerous. It exposes our inabilities that we can work on, develop and grow in. Let's look at the third construction worker's attitude.

He was building a cathedral. How big was it going to be, what were the dimensions, would he have enough bricks, where would all the money come from, how long will it take him, would he be able to see the completion of it in his life time? These and many other questions makes his "come from" dangerous. He could fail. Worse, he could look bad, be embarrassed and be shamed among his peers if he didn't have all the answers. However, he was connected to his WHY. His motivation came from within, not from circumstances.

The first two construction workers focused on themselves and what they could control without having to take risk, fail, look bad, or are embarrassed. The comfort zone is not a bad place, in fact without it we would be overwhelmed and eventually have a nervous break down. Imagine a young child of six years old at a mall lost from their parents. That is overwhelming and if that child doesn't find their parent's soon, they will be traumatized for a long time. Imagine the same child as a teenager at the mall without their parents, that's called heaven! Especially if they have their parent's credit card.

However if that same teenager grows up as an adult, single or married and continues to spend their recreational time at the same mall then that wouldn't serve them to mature and take on the responsibilities of a mature adult. It's not the comfort zone that is troubling, it's how long we stay in it. There is a healthy amount of time needed in our comfort zone to develop our character, produce courage, and to find familiarity. It only become toxic when we stay in our comfort zone longer then needed. The natural question then is how long do we need to be in our comfort zone? We need to leave our comfort zone when we have an invitation to become the best version of ourselves and that invitation is normally wrapped up in an opportunity to serve others.

At work, the invitation is to get a promotion in order to influence and lead others; that's building a cathedral since it's about serving others. But to get a promotion just to get a raise is like laying brick or building a wall, it's only about ourselves. In your relationships, you naturally serve those you love. You do the dishes for your spouse. On good days, you do the laundry, play with the kids, take the dog for a walk and when the moon is full, you will even clean the entire house. However, these actions are also within your comfort zone. The invitation out of your comfort zone is when there is a specific request made of you. Your children ask you to attend their play, sporting event, or worse, attend open house at school. They ask you to do something that you don't naturally want to do. Something that would take time away from something you rather do, like rest after work, have personal time cooking, mowing the yard, or reading a book in a bubble bath. There is a conflict of your time and you have to make a choice to step out of your comfort zone to serve others with the possibility of disappointing them, or play it safe and serve yourself. Serving others is what it will take to get you out of your comfort zone.

The second most significant event in my life was getting married. The first was when I made a life-defining decision on the ninth floor of the south tower, hence my company's name, 9 South. My defining moment was when I accepted that God had a bigger purpose for my life then achieving the American dream and my life was created to give myself away and serve others. Details of my transformation experience on the ninth floor, in the south tower coming soon in a future book. With the transformation of this defining moment, it led me to the next life-changing significant moment of my life, marrying Donna.

I didn't know my biological father and I had multiple stepfathers. All of my friends' parents were divorced and I vowel never to be married. Why would I go through the pain of divorce and the aftermath it left? I personally experienced the hardship, pain and suffering divorce left behind. Being grounded on my defining moment, I had hope. I knew I was created for more and marriage could work if I did it the way God intended, that we would serve one another and become one.

Donna and I just celebrated 20 years of marriage in New Zealand and Australia! However, it was a long road to 20 years. The first several years were full of ignorant bliss. Then after the honeymoon stage, I wanted out. She pressed all my buttons because she wasn't like me. Only if she was, how amazing that would have been, NOT! She was perfectly different and I resisted because she was a constant invitation out of my comfort zone. She would want to stay home and cuddle on the couch instead of exploring the city in the morning on Saturday. I can be home for an hour or two max, before I need to get out and do something. Donna can be home for a day or two before she is ready to leave the house. How opposite are we?

My invitation to get out of my comfort zone was meeting Donna's needs, focusing on her finding security in her comfort zone. Until I could do that, Donna too was hesitant to leave her comfort zone, as we all are. So someone had to step out of his or her comfort zone first. I wish I could tell you that it was me, but I think you already knew that it wasn't. For years, Donna stepped out of her comfort zone for me. Not till I did some serious self-development, received counseling, spiritual mentoring, and was tired and frustrated with our marriage not working that I stepped out of my comfort zone. In that process, which I'm sure felt like multiple lifetimes to Donna, I learned a phrase that summarizes how to get out of our comfort zone.

"When in doubt, focus out."

Chapter 7

Your Fears

"The only thing we have to fear, is fear itself."

Franklin D. Roosevelt

FEAR'S INVITATION

"Why would anyone want to get married?"

That was my question coming from a divorced family, not knowing my biological father, having multiple stepfathers and all of my friends' parents being divorced.

It was interesting timing that this question came about, like most questions that are an invitation for us to BE-come our commitment. I just had my defining moment a couple years before, when I realized I was created to have companionship with the Creator of Heaven and Earth through my daily choices, my passions, goals, and relationships.

I believed I would experience God's love through loving others and allowing others to love me. That was dangerous! That was not how I was raised. That was not what the education system taught me and the idea of experiencing God through others was never affirmed in my previous relationships' which could be describe by one word, abandonment.

You didn't buy this book to hear about my past relationships and the fear of moving forward into a committed relationship. You bought this book to become a six-figure coach. To have a lifestyle of transforming other's lives, to have a flexible schedule that allowed you to travel, have quality time with the family and love what you do. But in order for you to be this six-figure coach, you will not only have to hear my stories of abandonment, you will have to hear your client's story also.

Once we acknowledge our comfort zone, fear will kick in to keep us from having our committed vision, goal, or desire.

Then we will naturally resist, avoid, ignore or simply deny the fear we have and return to our comfort zone of control.

I want to give you another tool, another option to give your clients. Instead of seeing fear as negative emotion, embrace fear as a partner in your commitment of BE-ing a great leader, boss, spouse, parent, human, and coach.

Invite fear into your conversation as a partner who is inviting you into two commitments to get out of your comfort zone and achieving your goal. The first invitation is to acknowledge and honor the past. The second is to identify the obstacles that would prevent you to achieving the success you're committed to having.

First, embracing the fear to acknowledge and honor your past. Back to my story, I believed the further we could run from our past, the more successful we would be. That is a natural belief for people who came from a traumatic up brining that included verbal and physical violence. In my younger years I experience life where people were not taught or equipped how to engage with one another. So naturally, there were many miscommunications that led to frustration and eventually conflict.

The common ingredient that I saw that was not working was marriage. I experienced it personally living with a single mom and her multiple attempts to have marriages. I saw my single stepfather angry and bitter at relationships, even with his sibling and parents, not mentioning another broken marriage.

Why would these people in my life desire to be married? Didn't they, as adults, saw what I did as a child? It doesn't work! Why is there such a strong desire and need to be married? The financial strain of the divorce, emotional toll, spiritual damage, and destruction it leaves for the next generation. Didn't anyone see this besides me?

Then why now was there this desire in me? Why was the question or invitation becoming so strong? It is easier to live in my comfort zone at that time. To be a bachelor, only concerned about myself, my time, my entertainment, my passions, me, me, me, me. Fear flooded my mind, emotions, spirit, and every part of my existence.

I could do what many people do and allow the fear to drive me back into my comfort zone or I could do what leaders, world changers, and humans who realized they were created to be a gift to this world would do. I could embrace the fear, and partner with it to acknowledge my past and honor it.

FACES OF FEAR

Let's see the multiple faces of fear so that we know how to embrace it. Dr. Karl Albrecht says there are only *five basic fears*, out of which almost all of our other so-called fears are manufactured. These are:

1. **Extinction**—the fear of annihilation, of ceasing to exist. This is a more fundamental way to express it than just calling it "fear of death." The idea of *no longer being* arouses a *primary existential anxiety* in all normal humans. Consider that panicky feeling you get when you look over the edge of a high building.

2. **Mutilation**—the fear of losing any part of our precious bodily structure; the thought of having our body's boundaries invaded, or of losing the integrity of any

organ, body part, or natural function. Anxiety about animals, such as bugs, spiders, snakes, and other creepy things arises from fear of mutilation.

3. **Loss of Autonomy**—the fear of being immobilized, paralyzed, restricted, enveloped, overwhelmed, entrapped, imprisoned, smothered, or otherwise controlled by circumstances beyond our control. In physical form, it's commonly known as claustrophobia, but it also extends to our social interactions and relationships.

4. **Separation**—the fear of abandonment, rejection, and loss of connectedness; of *becoming a non-person*—not wanted, respected, or valued by anyone else. The "silent treatment," when imposed by a group, can have a devastating psychological effect on its target.

5. **Ego-death**—the fear of humiliation, shame, or any other mechanism of profound self-disapproval that threatens the *loss of integrity of the Self*; the fear of the shattering or disintegration of one's constructed sense of lovability, capability, and worthiness.

That's all—just those five. They can be thought of as forming a simple hierarchy, or "feararchy":

Fear Of:	**Ego Death**
Fear Of:	**Separation**
Fear Of:	**Loss of Autonomy**
Fear Of:	**Mutilation**
Fear Of:	**Extinction**

CREATING A PARTNERSHIP WITH FEAR

You see, most people who never leave their comfort zone will find a million pieces of evidence from their past to support their stance to stay single. And most of those evidences are great reasons not to move forward into a marriage. Though I had an emotionally violent up bringing, other people have experienced sexual abuse, physical abuse and other extreme events. Regardless of the events we can acknowledge them and honor them.

Step one: Acknowledge them. Acknowledging what happened to you is a healing process. It allows you, at a more mature age, to understand what happened, and that it hurt you, hence creating the current fear. Acknowledging it brings the event to light. It demystifies the power we have subscribed to it up to this point. It allows new evidence from our current maturity to see it in different ways. Simply put, acknowledging it, allows us to own it and it, the event, emotions, and pain, not to own us.

Step two: Honor the fear, regard it with great respect. It's counter intuitive, like most transformational work is. My fear of marriage came from a great place of my being that cared for me to be loved, respected, and happy. The fear drove me back to my comfort zone where I was safe and in control. Until I could see that the fear was my partner, not my enemy preventing me to achieve my goal of sharing my life with someone in a committed relationship, traditionally called marriage. Honoring my fear was embracing those things I brought to the light through acknowledging the issues. Instead of resisting our fears, we need to embrace them as partners. To see our fears as invitations to BEcoming our commitments.

THE SUCCESS OF THE PARTNERSHIP

I acknowledged the adults in my life that were to model for me marriage didn't have models themselves. They didn't have the tools of communications and resources of education counselors, pastors, and spiritual guides we have today. I acknowledged their broken marriage impact my relationship with the Creator. Then I honored my fear, not wanting to repeat the broken relationship cycle I experienced. I honored my fear inviting me to another path, direction, to a new possibility.

I basically flipped the script of my fears and found the opposite to be committed to that I have never seen since I've mostly focused on the past.

Feared in Marriage	**Committed to in marriage**
Abandonment	BE-ing committed
Conflict	Choosing not allowing the issue to be an issue
Losing my identity	Building on my identity
Divorce	Embracing it is real and focusing on serving
Imitating our parents	Acknowledging and honoring our parents and learning from them instead of resisting
Falling out of love	Committed to creating love and not be led by temporary emotions or circumstances
Unknown Future	Creating the future we desire
Finances	Living within the means of our vision

Partner with your fears then take the next step needed to accomplish your committed goal.

Chapter 8

You The Artist

Two roads diverged in a wood, and I took the less travelled by, and that has made all the difference.

Robert Frost

How will you get paid? How do you get customers? Will we be able to pay the monthly mortgage? How will we eat? More importantly, how will we eat consistently? These and a thousand other questions were asked before I took the leap to become a Corporate Coach.

In case you haven't figured out yet, I'm Asian American. We don't take risk. We are trained to conform, to adapt and not make waves. Become a lawyer, doctor, engineer, or something that has already been done and is safe.

When you get to know me, there is nothing safe about me. I am constantly pushing the envelope. I feel most alive when I'm outside of my comfort zone. Let me say that more accurately, I feel most purposeful. My life feels as it has significant meaning as I am out on a limb and fear rushes through my body. Maybe that is why I like to ride my motorcycle in southern California?

The point is you and I am a like in some degree if you're reading this book. You're not taking the road most traveled. You're looking for a lifestyle that empowers you to be an Artist, creating each day unique and different.

Robert Frost has poem about the road less taken. It goes like this: "Two roads diverged in a wood, and I took the one less traveled by, and that has made all the difference."

I say create a third new road, one no one has ever traveled because it is your road. It is paved with your personality, your commitments, your resources, and your passion. I'm being more extreme then Robert Frost to make a point, and to stretch the rubber band of your comfort zone. I want to invite you to start with a blank canvas creating your goal.

In order to be a successful six-figure coach, you have to apply this artistry to your life before coaching others to apply it to theirs.

I don't believe in A, B, C and 1, 2, 3 step formulas. That is the content of any program. I believe in the context, the way of BE-ing. So some of you by now are pissed at me and want me to give you the A, B, Cs of being a six-figure coach. I have an Accountability Coaching Model that has given me over six-figures annually, but without the way of BE-ing, regardless of the model, you won't be able to implement. With that said, here are a couple steps, not designed to follow linearly. Created to guide you and designed to be the core of creating your goal and having the flexibility for you to modify and adapt it to your unique personality.

To be an artist and create something out of nothing on your blank canvas

1. Leave the past

2. Live in the present

3. Create the future

LEAVE THE PAST BEHIND

One of the biggest barriers to achieving any dream is the S.E.E. I talked about in finding your WHY. If you haven't own your Significant Emotional Event - parents divorced, being discriminated against, or simply being different from others and experiencing rejection - then it will own you the rest of you life.

Universally, regardless of religion, I believe everyone will agree forgiveness is the foundation of letting the past be the past. Forgiveness doesn't mean you will forget the wound, it means you don't let that memory, emotions, or pain to own you in the present moment. You're able to talk about, share and remember the past events without any more emotional uprising.

I talk about the children making fun of me and discriminating against me now without the anger, shame or fear owning me. I share it from a different place, a "come from" that allows me to use my pain for other's gain. First I had to forgive the kids, their parents, and my parents for not blessing me to be different. Finally I had to forgive myself for taking their comments and creating a limiting story about myself that I lived in for years.

The process of leaving the past behind is not about forgetting. It's about owning. Owning the fact it happened, owning that it can be a gift, owning that you're in a different place and you can choose a different context the content is in now.

LIVE IN THE PRESENT

Believe it or not, most people live in the past more then they do in the present. College graduates live through their sport team's alma mater. Grown up adults who graduated 20 years ago still flock the stadiums of their college alma mater. The tell stories of how they use to play sports and the life style of a youthful carefree student.

To live in the present requires for us to first be free from the past pains and success. To literally start each day with a blank slate, new page of your chapter in life, and embrace the Holy Scriptures saying, "old things have gone, new things are here." I love the mall's legend telling us "You are here." This is where you take an honest inventory of your current reality. The life you created for yourself. It will speak to you if you listen. The money you make, career you have, friends, family, car you drive, everything you have up till now is feedback of your present life.

Own this and don't blame circumstances, your parents, the economy, or any other outside factors. If you embrace what you currently have mentally, physically, emotionally, spiritually, and relationally, then you will live in the present. I didn't say you had to like it, I said you just need to honestly embrace it. If you don't like what you currently have, then you're in the right place and we will create what you want next.

For now, live in the current moment. Sit in it for a while, experience your emotions, thoughts, and physical sensations. Is this where you want to be? If so, celebrate it. Celebrate that you created a life you enjoy, you're proud of and that bless the world. Be an example to others that they too can have a life like yours. Then continue being a model to others and set your next goal to widen your influence and become the best version of yourself.

The best sign that your living in the present is that you're fully aware of others and their emotions. I almost told you to be aware of their story, the stories we are telling everyone and ourselves every moment. However I choose to tell you to focus on their emotions. It is the catalyst to their story and actions. To be present in the moment, you're able to connect with people on a deeper level then their actions, you're connecting with their soul. You're present to be what is missing for them emotionally through a word of encouragement or a strong rebuke to detrimental actions. You're able to connect with them because you're present to your emotions and that frees you to be fully available to their emotions. When you connect like this with your clients, welcome to BE-ing a six-figure coach.

The last step of being an artist is creating the future. As a Christian I have friends who tell me there is only one Creator and that is God. I don't disagree and I'm not saying be God, I'm saying join your Creator in BE-ing responsible and owning your future by making the individual daily choices that moves you into the unprecedented future your committed to.

CREATE THE FUTURE

This is where you are free from your past, present to your current state and declare your unprecedented future. Declaring something that hasn't happened is creating your future. Declaring that you will lose 15lbs, when you have only lost 10lbs the most before is unprecedented. Declaring you will get married, take a relationship to a new level, or have children is creating the future. The future is waiting for you to create it! It is not predetermined for you and you just need to color in the number. It is a blank canvas waiting for your masterpiece to be revealed.

Until you believe this, the universe is waiting for your unique contribution to make this world its best, then you will conform to others color by number program. Instead, this is the level of maturity that separates leaders from followers. Leaders lead themselves first, then others. Lead yourself into your declared future, into your dream. It is scary, I agree, you haven't ever been there. You most likely won't have the resources needed because it is outside of your current control, comfort zone. And the journey of acquiring those resources and paving that new road is what make you alive, a contributor to society and a model for the next generation.

BOTTOM LINE

Being **responsible** for your unique expression is creating the future. You may do similar things other successful people who have gone before you like coaching. And you will never do it exactly like them. So don't try! Do it like you! Use other's success and mistakes to form your journey, except truly own your journey and create new success and failures for others to model after.

To create this future and BE uniquely yourself, you have to be **free** of comparison, failure, and judgment. You need to leave the past, exactly where it happened, in the past. Don't forget it, own it. Know that scar is a gift not a curse. When you own it, you will be able to use that experience, regardless how difficult it was to energize you for the present and future.

Then you will be a **contributor** to your unique expression, others, and the world. This is where the magic happens. This is the level that separates successful leaders from ordinary leaders. After we have identified our comfort zone and our fears that hold us back, we arrive at a pivot point. We either follow others color by number programs or we create our own destiny. Be an artist, create and receive the reward of freedom.

Chapter 9

Your Process

"The journey of a thousand miles begins with a single step."

Lao Tzu

How to BE a six-figure coach

It starts off with your way of BE-ing. Is your "come from" rooted in scarcity or abundance? When you wake up in the morning is it a repeat of yesterday, scarcity? Or is your morning a blank canvas waiting for you to create your goal with your unique diversity, abundance? If you're in scarcity, you're doing so you can have enough then one day you will become significant. Unfortunately, you know you can't do enough to have enough because someone always has more. Therefore, you can never become significant. This is what I call works salvation and it equals death; a separation of your dreams, relationships, and to your true unique identity.

When your "come from" is grounded in your BE-ing - BE-ing a great parent, great spouse, great friend, great child, great leader or simply a great human being - then you start to do from your BE-ing. You start to overflow from your commitment of who you are and what your committed to create. In fact you start doing less and each action you take is focused from your BE-ing. What ever you have resulting from your BE-ing and doing supports you. You have only what is needed and wanted in the moment to get you toward your committed goal. To have more would be distracting and diverting you from your committed goal. You will have exactly what you need and there is a contentment that follows.

A six-figure coach doesn't come from a magical formula of processed steps, they come from a committed way of BE-ing abundant!

NOW COACH

Now that you come from an abundant BE-ing any content will serve you to create results for your clients. The foundation to creating results is not found the desired goal. It is found in the current reality of your client.

CURRENT REALITY

What rewards are your clients benefiting from currently that will be difficult to surrender to get something new? What in their comfort zone is anchoring them from leaving and experiencing the unknown of their commitment? Start there. Identify what is giving them the most reward currently, celebrate it. Acknowledge all the hard work they have done to get where they are currently at. Then bless it and let it go. You're maturing, you have different desires and needs. Your dreams are including others and the world. You have to let go of what worked and embrace your new committed goal. An ancient scripture that reminds me of the natural maturity stages:

When I was a child, I spoke and thought and reasoned as a child. But when I grew up, I put away childish things.

I Corinthians 13.11

Your committed goal is calling you out of the old selfish rewards into a more mature reward that contributes to the world. Now its time to embrace and partner with our fears.

FEARS

Traditionally we see fear as something to avoid because it oppose a harm or threat to us. I want to invite you to consider that your fears are an invitation to expand who you are and become the best version of yourself. Fears are real and they are your body's way of protecting you from physical, mental, emotional, spiritual or relational harm. The fear reinforces the rewards of your comfort zone and supports your endeavors to build on those rewards until you're an expert in receiving that reward. You become in control of that reward and can access it at any time. Fear triggers you that others and circumstance are in control and that leaves you vulnerable.

Embrace that vulnerability and come from abundance that you're more then enough for that new experience. And then create what is wanted and needed in that moment for you to take the next steps toward your committed goal, BE an artist.

ARTIST CREATE

As simple as it sounds, the third step in coaching anyone into their committed goal is creating daily what is wanted and needed to take steps toward their dream. Artists come from a blank canvas daily and leave their unique expression on the canvas of life. Artists take responsibility for their contribution to their family, friends, colleagues and world daily. Artists inspire others through their risk of expressing their unique difference. Artists receive the rewards that only come from paving new ways for travel and not traveling on any other roads traveled.

The final step in creating value for your clients that consistently reward you six-figures is being responsible for each decision, action, and word you create.

NOW WHAT?

First, set a committed goal for yourself that invites you out of your comfort zone!

Example:

1. I will lose 20lbs by xyz date
2. I will make an additional $50,000 by end of Q2
3. I will reunite my relationship with my parents by xyz date

If you're going to create value that consistently generates you over six-figures a year, then you need to be comfortable with being uncomfortable. You have to keep experiencing identifying your comfort zone, partnering with your fear, and creating from a blank canvas daily.

If you need support, I have an Accountability Model that gives more of a framework that will support you to create a declaration step by step.

THIS IS WHY

I can tell you hundreds of stories of why I coach and how I have consistently made six-figures living a life style that only most dream of. I choose this one out of the hundreds of successes stories because I believe this success story aligns with your passion of becoming a six-figure coach.

Donna and I were living in the inner cities of Dallas. I was a city director of a non-profit committed to developing urban leaders. We live on the corner of Malcolm X and Martin Luther King. In any city in America, that intersection describes everything. We have built great relationships with the people in the community and one of the local couples was unfortunately addicted to drugs like most in the neighborhood. To support their addiction, he would do day labor work and she would sell herself. They lived in a shed they built behind an abandoned home. They were in their late forties, though they looked like they were in their sixties.

I asked Bobbie one day, "where is Sherri?" He said she was sick and she might be pregnant. I don't know if you ever been in Dallas, Texas during the summer? You can fry an egg on the sidewalk while you're getting a steam bath from the humidity. No human being, especially a pregnant one should be in a shed that had no air conditioning, much less no electricity or restroom.

Yes, we invited them to live with us and drew strong boundaries around their addiction. At the time we had three boys 4 years, 3 years and 1 year of age. There was something deep inside of us that was compelled to take this risk. To provide for others as we have been provided for. Bobby and Sherri stepped up into our invitation to be clean from drugs and a part of our family. Sherri's health and the baby was going well. Then a month later, Bobby went missing. Sherri wanted to go after him against my better judgment. Then they both were missing.

We grieved and questioned if we did the right thing, and were concerned if Sherri and the baby would be okay. After talking with everyone in the community, Bobby and Sherri were nowhere to be found.

A year later someone was knocking on my door, "Sabastian, how are you?" I said, "I'm sorry do I know you two?" It was Bobby and Sherri, they came back to say thank you! They had listened to all the coaching I gave them before they went missing and somewhere in their disappearance, they applied the principles. I was a rookie coach then and only gave them a couple fundamental coaching principles and those were enough for them to admit themselves into a drug rehab center. They were now leading the rehab and wanted to come back to say thank you. It is a moment in my life that I will never forget; it affirmed my passion to transform other people's lives through coaching. It was evidence that I could coach others, even when I didn't think I was doing anything right. It showed me how my work would not stop with those I coach and my impact would go beyond what I will ever know.

I give you this gift so you can see coaching isn't about a nice clean process. It's about getting messy; doing things you never have done in order to get something you never had. It's about doing what you know is right, though there is no precedent to your decisions or process. It's about allowing clients to own their own decisions, you standing to yours and them coming around to doing what's best for their vision. It's about being committed to the work of coaching even when your clients disappear on you. I give you this gift so you can see even when I began; I created value and learned from each client. I didn't get to become a six-figure coach overnight, I became a six-figure coach over a committed goal and you can too.

Now go out and change the world with a commitment to something bigger then your comfort zone, a six-figure salary, or a different life style. Be committed to becoming the best version of you and during the journey contributing to the most lives possible for them to be the biggest version of themselves. Start now with your committed goal that you will achieve in the next 90 days.

www.ingramcontent.com/pod-product-compliance
Lightning Source LLC
Chambersburg PA
CBHW061440180526
45170CB00004B/1498